VEGETARIAN AIR FRYER COOKBOOK

HEALTHY AND DELICIOUS MEATLESS RECIPES FOR EASY AIR FRYING

Lily Rose

TABLE OF CONTENT

TABLE OF CONTENT..2

1. AIR FRYER AVOCADO TOAST 4
2. CRISPY AIR FRYER HASH BROWNS 4
3. AIR FRYER FRENCH TOAST STICKS 5
4. FLUFFY AIR FRYER PANCAKES 6
5. AIR FRYER TOFU SCRAMBLE 7
6. AIR FRYER ZUCCHINI CHIPS 7
7. AIR FRYER CAULIFLOWER BUFFALO WINGS 8
8. CRISPY AIR FRYER MOZZARELLA STICKS 9
9. AIR FRYER JALAPEÑO POPPERS 10
10. AIR FRYER SWEET POTATO FRIES 11
11. AIR FRYER ONION RINGS 11
12. AIR FRYER GARLIC BREAD 12
13. AIR FRYER SAMOSAS 13
14. AIR FRYER FALAFEL 14
15. AIR FRYER CHICKPEAS 14
16. AIR FRYER BREAKFAST BURRITOS 15
17. AIR FRYER OATMEAL CUPS OF 16
18. AIR FRYER BLUEBERRY MUFFINS 17
19. AIR FRYER CINNAMON APPLE RINGS 18
20. AIR FRYER BANANA BREAD 18
21. AIR FRYER STUFFED PEPPERS 19
22. AIR FRYER VEGGIE BURGERS 20
23. AIR FRYER BBQ JACKFRUIT SANDWICHES 21
24. AIR FRYER EGGPLANT PARMESAN 22
25. AIR FRYER STUFFED PORTOBELLO MUSHROOMS 22
26. AIR FRYER GARLIC ROASTED BRUSSELS SPROUTS 23
27. AIR FRYER PARMESAN ASPARAGUS 24
28. AIR FRYER ROASTED CARROTS 25
29. AIR FRYER GREEN BEAN FRIES 25

- 30. AIR FRYER SPICED POTATO WEDGES 26
- 31. AIR FRYER CORN ON THE COB 27
- 32. AIR FRYER CRISPY TOFU BITES 27
- 33. AIR FRYER ROASTED CHICKPEA SALAD 28
- 34. AIR FRYER STUFFED GRAPE LEAVES 29
- 35. AIR FRYER CHEESY CAULIFLOWER BITES 30
- 36. AIR FRYER FRIED ICE CREAM 30
- 37. AIR FRYER PUMPKIN SPICE DONUTS 31
- 38. AIR FRYER COCONUT MACAROONS 32
- 39. AIR FRYER CINNAMON SUGAR DONUTS 33
- 40. AIR FRYER BANANA CHIPS 34
- 41. AIR FRYER STRAWBERRY SHORTCAKE 34
- 42. AIR FRYER S'MORES 35
- 43. AIR FRYER VEGAN TACOS 36
- 44. AIR FRYER TEMPEH STIR FRY 37
- 45. AIR FRYER CHOCOLATE LAVA CAKE 38
- 46. AIR FRYER CHURROS 39
- 47. AIR FRYER APPLE HAND PIES 39
- 48. AIR FRYER BROWNIES 40
- 49. AIR FRYER PEANUT BUTTER COOKIES 41
- 50. ZEMIAKOVÝ GULÁŠ S ZELENINOU (POTATO GOULASH WITH VEGETABLES) 41
- 51. KUSHARI DELIGHT 42
- 52. FAVA BEAN FALAFEL 43
- 53. ALEXANDRIA SEAFOOD STEW 44
- 54. EGYPTIAN LENTIL SOUP 45
- 55. KOFTA KEBABS WITH TZATZIKI 45
- 56. HAWAWSHI - MEAT-STUFFED PITA 46
- 57. MOLOKHIA GREEN SOUP 47
- 58. BASBOUSA - SEMOLINA CAKE 48
- 59. TAHINI HONEY ROASTED CARROTS 49
- 60. SHISH TAOUK SKEWERS 50

1. AIR FRYER AVOCADO TOAST

Prep Time: 5 mins
Cook Time: 4 mins
Total Time: 9 mins
Servings: 2

Ingredients:

- 2 slices of bread (sourdough or whole grain)
- 1 ripe avocado
- ½ tsp lemon juice
- ¼ tsp salt
- ¼ tsp black pepper
- ½ tsp red pepper flakes (non-compulsory)
- 1 tbsp olive oil (non-compulsory, for crispy toast)

Instructions:

1. Set the air fryer's temperature to 370°F, or 188°C.
2. To make the bread more crispier, lightly brush it with olive oil.
3. Put the bread in the basket of the air fryer and toast it for three to four mins, or up to it is golden brown.
4. In the meantime, mash the avocado with salt, pepper, and lemon juice.
5. Cover the toasted bread with the avocado Mixture.
6. Add your preferred toppings or red pepper flakes on top. Serve right away.

Nutrition (Per Serving):

Cals: 220, Carbs: 24g

Protein: 5gm, Fat: 12g

Fiber: 6g

2. CRISPY AIR FRYER HASH BROWNS

Prep Time: 10 mins
Cook Time: 15 mins
Total Time: 25 mins
Servings: 4

Ingredients:

- 2 Big potatoes, shredded
- 1 tbsp olive oil

- ½ tsp salt
- ½ tsp black pepper
- ½ tsp garlic powder
- ½ tsp onion powder

Instructions:

1. Preheat the air fryer to 375°F, or 190°C.
2. Take out any remaining liquid from the crushed potatoes with a towel.
3. In a bowl, combine together the potatoes, olive oil, salt, pepper, onion powder, and garlic powder.
4. Spread a thin layer of potatoes in the air fryer basket.
5. Cook for 12 to 15 mins, shaking halfway through, up to crispy and browned.
6. Serve hot with the dipping sauce of your choice.

Nutrition (Per Serving):

Cals: 130, Carbs: 27g

Protein: 2g, Fat: 3g

Fiber: 2g

3. AIR FRYER FRENCH TOAST STICKS

Prep Time: 5 mins
Cook Time: 8 mins
Total Time: 13 mins
Servings: 4

Ingredients:

- 4 slices of bread, slice into strips
- 2 eggs
- ½ cup milk
- 1 tsp vanilla extract
- 1 tsp cinnamon
- 1 tbsp sugar
- Cooking spray

Instructions:

1. Preheat the air fryer to 375°F (190°C).
2. In a bowl, whisk eggs, milk, vanilla, cinnamon, and sugar.
3. Dip the bread sticks into the Mixture, coating both sides.
4. Spray the air fryer basket with cooking spray.

5. Arrange the sticks in a single layer and cook for 8 mins, flipping halfway.
6. Serve with maple syrup or powdered sugar.

Nutrition (Per Serving):

Cals: 190, Carbs: 30g

Protein: 6g, Fat: 4g

Fiber: 2g

4. FLUFFY AIR FRYER PANCAKES

Prep Time: 5 mins
Cook Time: 8 mins
Total Time: 13 mins
Servings: 4

Ingredients:

- 1 cup all-purpose flour
- 1 tbsp sugar
- 1 tsp baking powder
- ½ tsp baking soda
- ¼ tsp salt
- ¾ cup milk
- 1 egg
- 1 tbsp dilute butter
- ½ tsp vanilla extract

Instructions:

1. Set the air fryer's temperature to 320°F, or 160°C.
2. Combine the flour, sugar, baking soda, baking powder, and salt in a bowl.
3. Beat the egg, milk, vanilla, and dilute butter in a separate basin.
4. Combine the dry and wet ingredients together up to they are smooth.
5. Grease a mini pan that is suitable to use in an air fryer, then ladle dough into it (about ¼ cup for every pancake).
6. Air fry till golden brown, 6 to 8 mins.
7. Serve with fruit and syrup.

Nutrition (Per Serving):

Cals: 210, Carbs: 32g

Protein: 6g, Fat: 6g

Fiber: 1g

5. AIR FRYER TOFU SCRAMBLE

Prep Time: 5 mins
Cook Time: 10 mins
Total Time: 15 mins
Servings: 2

Ingredients:

- 1 block (14 oz) firm tofu, cut up
- 1 tbsp olive oil
- ½ tsp turmeric
- ½ tsp garlic powder
- ½ tsp onion powder
- ½ tsp salt
- ¼ tsp black pepper
- 1 tbsp nutritional yeast (non-compulsory)

Instructions:

1. Set the air fryer's temperature to 375°F, or 190°C.
2. Combine the cut up tofu, spices, and olive oil in a bowl.
3. Fill the basket of the air fryer with the tofu Mixture.
4. Cook, shaking halfway through, for 8 to 10 mins.
5. Serve hot with veggies or toast.

Nutrition (Per Serving):

Cals: 180, Carbs: 6g

Protein: 16g, Fat: 12g

Fiber: 3g

6. AIR FRYER ZUCCHINI CHIPS

Prep Time: 10 mins
Cook Time: 10 mins
Total Time: 20 mins
Servings: 4

Ingredients:

- 1 medium zucchini, split into thin rounds

- 1/2 cup panko breadcrumbs
- 1/4 cup finely grated Parmesan cheese
- 1/2 tsp garlic powder
- 1/2 tsp paprika
- 1/2 tsp salt
- 1/4 tsp black pepper
- 1 Big egg
- Cooking spray

Instructions:

1. Set the air fryer's temperature to 375°F, or 190°C.
2. Whisk together the egg in a bowl.
3. Combine the breadcrumbs, paprika, garlic powder, Parmesan cheese, salt, and pepper in a separate bowl.
4. Coat every zucchini slice with the breadcrumb Mixture after dipping it into the egg.
5. Line the basket in the air fryer with a single layer of the breaded zucchini slices. Apply cooking spray sparingly.
6. Air fried up to golden and crispy, 8 to 10 mins, turning halfway through.
7. Serve right away with your preferred dipping sauce.

Nutrition (Per Serving):

Cals: 120, Protein: 6g

Carbs: 15g

Fat: 4g, Fiber: 2g

7. AIR FRYER CAULIFLOWER BUFFALO WINGS

Prep Time: 15 mins
Cook Time: 15 mins
Total Time: 30 mins
Servings: 4

Ingredients:

- 1 mini head of cauliflower, slice into florets
- 1/2 cup all-purpose flour
- 1/2 cup water
- 1 tsp garlic powder
- 1/2 tsp salt
- 1/2 tsp black pepper
- 1 cup panko breadcrumbs

- 1/2 cup buffalo sauce
- 1 tbsp dilute butter

Instructions:

1. Set the air fryer's temperature to 375°F, or 190°C.
2. To prepare a batter, combine flour, water, salt, pepper, and garlic powder in a bowl.
3. Coat the cauliflower florets with panko breadcrumbs after dipping them into the batter.
4. Place in the air fryer basket in a single layer and cook for 12 to 15 mins, shaking the basket occasionally.
5. Add the cooked cauliflower to the buffalo sauce after combining it with dilute butter.
6. For added crispiness, put the air fryer back in for two to three more mins.
7. Serve hot with blue cheese or ranch dressing.

Nutrition (Per Serving):

Cals: 170, Protein: 5g

Carbs: 25g

Fat: 5g, Fiber: 3g

8. CRISPY AIR FRYER MOZZARELLA STICKS

Prep Time: 15 mins (+ freezing time)
Cook Time: 8 mins
Total Time: 23 mins
Servings: 4

Ingredients:

- 8 mozzarella string cheese sticks, halved
- 1/2 cup all-purpose flour
- 2 Big eggs, beaten
- 1 cup panko breadcrumbs
- 1/2 tsp garlic powder
- 1/2 tsp Italian seasoning
- 1/4 tsp salt
- Cooking spray

Instructions:

1. Put the mozzarella sticks in the freezer for at least half an hr.
2. Fill one bowl with flour, another with beaten eggs, and a third with breadcrumbs, salt, Italian seasoning, and garlic powder.
3. Dip every mozzarella stick in breadcrumbs, egg, and flour. For additional coating, repeat.

4. For another half hr, freeze.
5. Set the air fryer's temperature to 375°F, or 190°C.
6. Spray the basket with a little cooking spray and arrange the sticks in a single layer.
7. For 6 to 8 mins, air fry, rotating halfway through.
8. Serve with marinara sauce right away.

Nutrition (Per Serving):

Cals: 210, Protein: 12g

Carbs: 18g

Fat: 10g, Fiber: 1g

9. AIR FRYER JALAPEÑO POPPERS

Prep Time: 10 mins
Cook Time: 8 mins
Total Time: 18 mins
Servings: 4

Ingredients:

- 6 jalapeños, halved and deseeded
- 4 oz cream cheese, melted
- 1/2 cup shredded cheddar cheese
- 1/4 tsp garlic powder
- 1/4 tsp salt
- 1/4 tsp black pepper
- 4 slices bacon, slice in half
- Cooking spray

Instructions:

1. Set the air fryer's temperature to 375°F, or 190°C.
2. Combine the cream cheese, cheddar cheese, salt, pepper, and garlic powder in a bowl.
3. Fill the cheese Mixture into every side of a jalapeño.
4. Secure every filled jalapeño with a toothpick after wrapping it with a slice of bacon.
5. Place in the basket of the air fryer and lightly mist with cooking spray.
6. The bacon Must be crispy after 7 to 8 mins in the air fryer.
7. Serve right away.

Nutrition (Per Serving):

Cals: 180, Protein: 6g

Carbs: 4g

Fat: 15g, Fiber: 1g

10. AIR FRYER SWEET POTATO FRIES

Prep Time: 10 mins
Cook Time: 15 mins
Total Time: 25 mins
Servings: 4

Ingredients:

- 2 medium sweet potatoes, peel off and slice into fries
- 1 tbsp olive oil
- 1/2 tsp salt
- 1/2 tsp paprika
- 1/2 tsp garlic powder
- 1/4 tsp black pepper

Instructions:

1. Set the air fryer's temperature to 375°F, or 190°C.
2. Combine sweet potato fries, olive oil, salt, paprika, black pepper, and garlic powder in a bowl.
3. Put the fries in the basket of the air fryer in a single layer.
4. Shake the basket halfway through and air fry for 12 to 15 mins, or up to crispy.
5. Serve with your preferred dipping sauce right away.

Nutrition (Per Serving):

Cals: 130, Protein: 2g

Carbs: 25g

Fat: 3g, Fiber: 4g

11. AIR FRYER ONION RINGS

Prep Time: 15 mins
Cook Time: 10 mins
Total Time: 25 mins
Servings: 4

Ingredients:

- 1 Big onion, split into rings
- 1 cup all-purpose flour

- 1 tsp paprika
- 1 tsp garlic powder
- ½ tsp salt
- ½ tsp black pepper
- 2 eggs, beaten
- 1 cup panko breadcrumbs
- Cooking spray

Instructions:

1. Set the air fryer's temperature to 375°F, or 190°C.
2. Combine the flour, salt, pepper, garlic powder, and paprika in a bowl.
3. Coat every onion ring with panko breadcrumbs after dipping it first in the flour Mixture and then in the beaten eggs.
4. Arrange the rings in a single layer after applying cooking spray to the air fryer basket.
5. Air fried up to golden brown and crispy, turning halfway through, 8 to 10 mins.
6. Serve with your preferred dipping sauce right away.

Nutrition (Per Serving):

Cals: 220, Carbs: 30g

Protein: 6g, Fat: 8g

12. AIR FRYER GARLIC BREAD

Prep Time: 5 mins
Cook Time: 5 mins
Total Time: 10 mins
Servings: 4

Ingredients:

- 4 slices of bread (French or Italian)
- 4 tbsp butter, dilute
- 3 cloves garlic, chop-up
- 1 tbsp fresh parsley, chop-up
- ¼ tsp salt
- ¼ tsp black pepper
- ¼ cup finely grated Parmesan (non-compulsory)

Instructions:

1. Set the air fryer's temperature to 175°C (350°F).
2. Combine the dilute butter, parsley, salt, pepper, and chop-up garlic in a bowl.

3. Evenly cover every piece of bread with the Mixture, and if desired, sprinkle Parmesan on top.
4. Cook for 4 to 5 mins, or up to golden brown, in the air fryer basket.
5. Warm up and serve.

Nutrition (Per Serving):

Cals: 180, Carbs: 18g

Protein: 4g, Fat: 10g

13. AIR FRYER SAMOSAS

Prep Time: 20 mins
Cook Time: 15 mins
Total Time: 35 mins
Servings: 6

Ingredients:

- 1 cup mashed potatoes
- ½ cup peas
- ½ tsp cumin seeds
- ½ tsp garam masala
- ½ tsp turmeric
- ½ tsp salt
- ½ tsp chili powder
- 1 tbsp chop-up cilantro
- 6 samosa wrappers or phyllo dough
- Cooking spray

Instructions:

1. Set the air fryer's temperature to 375°F, or 190°C.
2. Mashed potatoes, peas, turmeric, garam masala, cumin seeds, salt, chili powder, and cilantro Must all be combined in a bowl.
3. After filling every wrapper with the contents, fold it into a triangle and use water to seal the edges.
4. Apply cooking spray to the samosas sparingly.
5. Air fried up to golden brown and crispy, turning halfway through, 12 to 15 mins.
6. Serve with tamarind sauce or mint chutney.

Nutrition (Per Serving):

Cals: 150, Carbs: 22g

Protein: 4g, Fat: 5g

14. AIR FRYER FALAFEL

Prep Time: 10 mins
Cook Time: 15 mins
Total Time: 25 mins
Servings: 4

Ingredients:

- 1 can (15 oz) chickpeas, drained
- ½ cup fresh parsley
- 2 cloves garlic
- ½ tsp cumin
- ½ tsp coriander
- ¼ tsp salt
- ¼ tsp black pepper
- 2 tbsp flour
- 1 tbsp olive oil
- Cooking spray

Instructions:

1. Set the air fryer's temperature to 375°F, or 190°C.
2. Combine the chickpeas, parsley, garlic, cumin, coriander, salt, and pepper in a mixer.
3. Add flour and combine up to little balls form.
4. Place in the basket of the air fryer after lightly spraying with cooking spray.
5. Halfway through, shake the basket. Air fry for 12 to 15 mins.
6. Add tahini sauce on the side.

Nutrition (Per Serving):

Cals: 160, Carbs: 25g

Protein: 6g, Fat: 5g

15. AIR FRYER CHICKPEAS

Prep Time: 5 mins
Cook Time: 12 mins
Total Time: 17 mins
Servings: 4

Ingredients:

- 1 can (15 oz) chickpeas, drained and patted dry
- 1 tbsp olive oil
- ½ tsp garlic powder
- ½ tsp paprika
- ½ tsp salt
- ¼ tsp black pepper

Instructions:

1. Set the air fryer's temperature to 375°F, or 190°C.
2. Combine chickpeas, olive oil, paprika, garlic powder, salt, and pepper in a bowl.
3. Line the basket of the air fryer with a single layer of chickpeas.
4. Halfway through, shake the basket. Air fry for 12 to 15 mins.
5. Before serving, let it cool somewhat.

Nutrition (Per Serving):

Cals: 120, Carbs: 18g

Protein: 5g, Fat: 4g

16. AIR FRYER BREAKFAST BURRITOS

Prep Time: 10 mins
Cook Time: 8 mins
Total Time: 18 mins
Servings: 4 burritos

Ingredients

- 4 Big flour tortillas
- 4 eggs
- 1/2 cup shredded cheddar cheese
- 1/2 cup cooked breakfast sausage (cut up) or diced ham
- 1/4 cup diced bell peppers (red or green)
- 1/4 cup diced onions
- Salt and pepper, as needed
- Cooking spray or a tsp of oil

Instructions

1. Preheat and Get Ready: Set your air fryer's temperature to 360°F (182°C). Apply a tiny amount of cooking spray to a bowl that fits inside your air fryer.
2. Cooking Filling: Saute the chop-up bell peppers and onions in a pan over medium heat (or in the microwave) up to they are tender. Stir in the shredded ham or sausage. Add the

eggs to the pan after whisking them with salt and pepper. Just scramble the eggs by gently stirring them.
3. Put the burritos together: Spoon a uniform quantity of the egg Mixture into the middle of a flattened tortilla. Top with a mini amount of cheese. Fold the tortilla's sides in as you roll it into a burrito.
4. Air Fry: Put the burritos in the basket of the air fryer, seam side down. Cook, flipping halfway through, up to the tortilla is golden and crisp, approximately 8 mins.
5. Serve: Gently take out, slice in half if you'd like, and serve warm.

NUTRITION INFO (per burrito, approx.)

Cals: 280–320, Protein: 15–18g

Carbs: 30–35g

Fat: 12–15g

17. AIR FRYER OATMEAL CUPS OF

Prep Time: 5 mins
Cook Time: 12 mins
Total Time: 17 mins
Servings: 6 cups of

Ingredients

- 1 cup rolled oats
- 1/2 cup milk (dairy or non-dairy)
- 1 egg
- 1 mashed banana (about 1/2 cup)
- 1/4 cup chop-up berries (blueberries or raspberries)
- 1 tbsp honey or maple syrup
- 1/2 tsp baking powder
- A pinch of salt
- Non-compulsory: 1/4 tsp cinnamon

Instructions

1. Set your air fryer's temperature to 350°F (175°C).
2. Add the oats, milk, egg, mashed banana, honey, baking powder, salt, and cinnamon to a bowl. Add berries and stir gently.
3. Fill Cups of: Using a spoon, evenly distribute the Mixture into muffin cups of that are ovenproof or silicone.
4. Air Fry: Put the cups of in the basket of an air fryer and cook for 12 mins, or up to the tops are somewhat browned and firm.

5. Cool & Serve: Before removing the oatmeal cups of from the cups of, let them to cool somewhat. Savor it as a quick snack or breakfast.

NUTRITION INFO (per cup, approx.)

Cals: 130–150, Protein: 4–5g

Carbs: 25–28g

Fat: 2–3g

18. AIR FRYER BLUEBERRY MUFFINS

Prep Time: 10 mins
Cook Time: 12 mins
Total Time: 22 mins
Servings: 6 muffins

Ingredients

- 1 cup all-purpose flour
- 1/3 cup granulated sugar
- 1/2 tsp baking powder
- 1/4 tsp baking soda
- A pinch of salt
- 1/2 cup blueberries (fresh or refrigerate)
- 1/2 cup plain yogurt or milk
- 1 egg
- 2 tbsp dilute butter or oil
- 1/2 tsp vanilla extract

Instructions

1. Set the air fryer's temperature to 350°F (175°C).
2. Dry Combine: Combine flour, sugar, baking soda, baking powder, and salt in a medium-sized basin and combine to combine.
3. Wet Combine: Beat the egg, yogurt, dilute butter, and vanilla extract in a separate dish.
4. Combine: Gently fold in the blueberries after combining the wet ingredients with the dry ones up to just combined.
5. Fill Muffin Cups of: Using a spoon, fill silicone muffin cups of about two thirds of the way to the top.
6. A toothpick placed in the center of the muffin cups of Must come out clean after 12 mins of cooking in the air fryer basket.
7. Cool & Serve: Before consuming, let the muffins cool for a few mins.

NUTRITION INFO (per muffin, approx.)

Cals: 150–170, Protein: 4–5g

Carbs: 25–28g

Fat: 5–7g

19. AIR FRYER CINNAMON APPLE RINGS

Prep Time: 10 mins
Cook Time: 15 mins
Total Time: 25 mins
Servings: 4 servings

Ingredients

- 2 Big apples (firm varieties like Honeycrisp or Gala)
- 2 tbsp unsalted butter, dilute
- 2 tbsp brown sugar
- 1 tsp ground cinnamon
- A pinch of salt
- Non-compulsory: 1 tbsp lemon juice

Instructions

1. Set your air fryer's temperature to 360°F (182°C).
2. To prepare the apples, core them and slice them into rings that are 1/4 inch thick. To keep them from browning, you can drizzle them with a little lemon juice if you like.
3. Coat: Combine the salt, cinnamon, brown sugar, and dilute butter in a basin. Apply the Mixture to both sides of every apple ring.
4. Air Fry: Put the apple rings in the basket of the air fryer in a single layer. Cook up to soft and caramelized, turning halfway through, 15 mins.
5. Serve: Gently take out and serve warm as a dessert or side dish.

NUTRITION INFO (per serving, approx.)

Cals: 90–110, Protein: 0.5–1g

Carbs: 22–26g

Fat: 3–4g

20. AIR FRYER BANANA BREAD

Prep Time: 15 mins
Cook Time: 30 mins

Total Time: 45 mins
Servings: 8 slices

Ingredients

- 2–3 ripe bananas, mashed (about 1 cup)
- 1 1/2 cups of all-purpose flour
- 1/2 cup granulated sugar
- 1/4 cup brown sugar
- 1 egg, lightly beaten
- 1/3 cup dilute butter
- 1 tsp baking soda
- 1/2 tsp salt
- 1/2 tsp vanilla extract
- Non-compulsory: 1/2 cup chop-up walnuts or chocolate chips

Instructions

1. Set your air fryer's temperature to 320°F (160°C).
2. Combine Dry Ingredients: Whisk the flour, baking soda, and salt in a Big basin.
3. Combine Wet Ingredients: Put the sugars, egg, dilute butter, vanilla essence, and mashed bananas in a separate dish.
4. Combine: Just combine the wet and dry components by stirring them together. If using, fold in chocolate chips or walnuts.
5. Get the pan ready: A mini loaf pan that will fit in your air fryer Must be greased.
6. Bake: Fill the loaf pan with batter and put it in the air fryer. A toothpick inserted in the center Must come out clean after 30 mins of baking.
7. Let the banana bread cool somewhat before slicing it.

NUTRITION INFO (per slice, approx.)

Cals: 190–220, Protein: 3–4g

Carbs: 30–35g

21. AIR FRYER STUFFED PEPPERS

Prep Time: 15 mins
Cook Time: 15 mins
Total Time: 30 mins
Servings: 4

Ingredients:

- 4 bell peppers (halved and deseeded)
- 1 cup cooked rice

- ½ lb ground turkey or plant-based alternative
- 1 mini onion, diced
- 2 cloves garlic, chop-up
- 1 cup tomato sauce
- ½ cup shredded mozzarella cheese
- 1 tsp Italian seasoning
- ½ tsp salt
- ½ tsp black pepper
- Olive oil spray

Instructions:

1. Set the air fryer's temperature to 375°F, or 190°C.
2. Add the onion and garlic to a pan over medium heat and cook up to they are tender.
3. Cook till browned after adding ground turkey (or a plant-based substitute).
4. Add the cooked rice, tomato sauce, salt, pepper, and Italian seasoning. Simmer for three mins.
5. Spoon the Mixture into every half of a bell pepper and sprinkle mozzarella cheese on top.
6. Apply a little layer of olive oil to the air fryer basket. Stuffed peppers Must be put inside.
7. The peppers Must be soft and the cheese Must be dilute after 10 to 12 mins of air fry time.
8. Warm up and dig in!

Nutrition (Per Serving):

Cals: 250, Protein: 18g

Carbs: 28g, Fat: 8g

Fiber: 5g

22. AIR FRYER VEGGIE BURGERS

Prep Time: 10 mins
Cook Time: 12 mins
Total Time: 22 mins
Servings: 4

Ingredients:

- 1 can (15 oz) black beans, drained and mashed
- ½ cup breadcrumbs
- ¼ cup finely grated carrots
- ¼ cup lightly chop-up onion
- 1 tsp garlic powder
- 1 tsp smoked paprika

- 1 tbsp soy sauce
- 1 tbsp ground flaxseed + 3 tbsp water (egg substitute)
- Olive oil spray

Instructions:

1. Combine the flaxseed and water in a dish and leave for five mins.
2. In a bowl, combine all the ingredients and stir thoroughly. Make four patties.
3. Turn the air fryer on to 375°F, or 190°C.
4. Place patties in the air fryer basket, lightly spray the basket, and then drizzle the tops with olive oil.
5. Cook, flipping halfway through, for 10 to 12 mins.
6. Top with your preferred toppings and serve on buns.

Nutrition (Per Patty):

Cals: 180, Protein: 7g

Carbs: 30g, Fat: 3g

Fiber: 8g

23. AIR FRYER BBQ JACKFRUIT SANDWICHES

Prep Time: 10 mins
Cook Time: 10 mins
Total Time: 20 mins
Servings: 4

Ingredients:

- 1 can (20 oz) young jackfruit, drained and shredded
- ½ cup BBQ sauce
- 1 tsp smoked paprika
- ½ tsp garlic powder
- ½ tsp onion powder
- 4 sandwich buns
- Olive oil spray

Instructions:

1. Set the air fryer's temperature to 375°F, or 190°C.
2. Combine the jackfruit, paprika, onion powder, garlic powder, and BBQ sauce in a bowl.
3. Spread out the jackfruit and lightly spray the air fryer basket.
4. Air fry till just crispy, 8 to 10 mins, shaking halfway through.
5. Serve with pickles or coleslaw on buns.

Nutrition (Per Sandwich):

Cals: 250, Protein: 4g

Carbs: 45g, Fat: 3g

Fiber: 5g

24. AIR FRYER EGGPLANT PARMESAN

Prep Time: 15 mins
Cook Time: 12 mins
Total Time: 27 mins
Servings: 4

Ingredients:

- 1 Big eggplant, split into ½-inch rounds
- 1 cup breadcrumbs
- ½ cup finely grated Parmesan cheese
- 1 tsp Italian seasoning
- ½ tsp garlic powder
- 2 eggs, beaten (or plant-based alternative)
- 1 cup marinara sauce
- ½ cup shredded mozzarella cheese
- Olive oil spray

Instructions:

1. Set the air fryer's temperature to 375°F, or 190°C.
2. In a bowl, combine breadcrumbs, garlic powder, Parmesan, and Italian seasoning.
3. Coat every eggplant slice with the breadcrumb Mixture after dipping it in beaten egg.
4. Arrange the eggplant slices in a single layer in the air fryer basket after lightly spraying it.
5. After 8 mins in the air fryer, turn and continue cooking for 4 more mins.
6. Add mozzarella and marinara sauce on top, then air fried for an additional two mins.
7. Warm up and serve.

Nutrition (Per Serving):

Cals: 220, Protein: 12g

Carbs: 30g, Fat: 8g

Fiber: 6g

25. AIR FRYER STUFFED PORTOBELLO MUSHROOMS

Prep Time: 10 mins
Cook Time: 12 mins
Total Time: 22 mins
Servings: 4

Ingredients:

- 4 Big portobello mushrooms, stems take outd
- ½ cup cream cheese (or dairy-free alternative)
- ¼ cup finely grated Parmesan (or nutritional yeast)
- 1 clove garlic, chop-up
- ½ tsp Italian seasoning
- ¼ cup chop-up spinach
- ¼ cup breadcrumbs
- Olive oil spray

Instructions:

1. Set the air fryer's temperature to 375°F, or 190°C.
2. Combine spinach, Parmesan, garlic, Italian seasoning, and cream cheese in a bowl.
3. Sprinkle the breadcrumbs on top after spooning the Mixture into the mushroom caps.
4. Place the mushrooms in the air fryer basket after lightly spraying it.
5. The mushrooms Must be soft and the filling Must be brown after 10 to 12 mins of air fry time.
6. Warm up and serve.

Nutrition (Per Stuffed Mushroom):

Cals: 160, Protein: 8g

Carbs: 10g, Fat: 10g

Fiber: 3g

26. AIR FRYER GARLIC ROASTED BRUSSELS SPROUTS

Prep Time: 10 mins
Cook Time: 12 mins
Total Time: 22 mins
Servings: 4

Ingredients:

- 1 lb Brussels sprouts, trimmed and halved
- 2 tbsp olive oil

- 3 cloves garlic, chop-up
- ½ tsp salt
- ¼ tsp black pepper
- ½ tsp red pepper flakes (non-compulsory)
- 1 tbsp balsamic vinegar (non-compulsory)

Instructions:

1. Set the air fryer's temperature to 375°F, or 190°C.
2. Combine the Brussels sprouts, salt, black pepper, red pepper flakes, garlic, and olive oil in a bowl.
3. Arrange the Brussels sprouts in a single layer within the air fryer basket.
4. Halfway through the 12-min cooking time, shake the basket.
5. Before serving, drizzle with balsamic vinegar, if using.

Nutrition (per serving):

Cals: 120, Carbs: 10g

Protein: 3g, Fat: 8g

Fiber: 4g

27. AIR FRYER PARMESAN ASPARAGUS

Prep Time: 5 mins
Cook Time: 7 mins
Total Time: 12 mins
Servings: 4

Ingredients:

- 1 bunch asparagus, trimmed
- 1 tbsp olive oil
- ¼ tsp salt
- ¼ tsp black pepper
- ¼ cup finely grated Parmesan cheese
- ½ tsp garlic powder

Instructions:

1. Set the air fryer's temperature to 400°F, or 200°C.
2. Add garlic powder, salt, black pepper, and olive oil to the asparagus.
3. Place the asparagus in a single layer within the air fryer basket.
4. Shake the basket midway through the 7-min cooking time.
5. Before serving, top with Parmesan cheese.

Nutrition (per serving):

Cals: 90, Carbs: 5g

Protein: 4g, Fat: 6g

Fiber: 2g

28. AIR FRYER ROASTED CARROTS

Prep Time: 5 mins
Cook Time: 15 mins
Total Time: 20 mins
Servings: 4

Ingredients:

- 4 Big carrots, peel off and slice into sticks
- 1 tbsp olive oil
- ½ tsp salt
- ¼ tsp black pepper
- ½ tsp paprika
- ½ tsp garlic powder
- 1 tsp honey (non-compulsory)

Instructions:

1. Set the air fryer's temperature to 375°F, or 190°C.
2. Add paprika, garlic powder, salt, black pepper, and olive oil to the carrot sticks.
3. Arrange in a single layer in the air fryer basket.
4. Cook, shaking the basket halfway through, for 15 mins.
5. Before serving, drizzle with honey, if using.

Nutrition (per serving):

Cals: 80, Carbs: 12g

Protein: 1g, Fat: 4g

Fiber: 3g

29. AIR FRYER GREEN BEAN FRIES

Prep Time: 10 mins
Cook Time: 8 mins
Total Time: 18 mins
Servings: 4

Ingredients:

- 1 lb fresh green beans, trimmed
- ½ cup panko breadcrumbs
- ¼ cup finely grated Parmesan cheese
- 1 tsp garlic powder
- ½ tsp salt
- ¼ tsp black pepper
- 2 eggs, beaten
- Cooking spray

Instructions:

1. Set the air fryer's temperature to 400°F, or 200°C.
2. Combine the panko breadcrumbs, Parmesan cheese, salt, black pepper, and garlic powder in a bowl.
3. Coat the green beans with the breadcrumb Mixture after dipping them in the beaten eggs.
4. Arrange in a single layer in the air fryer basket and lightly mist with cooking spray.
5. Shake the basket halfway during the 8-min cooking time.

Nutrition (per serving):

Cals: 130, Carbs: 14g

Protein: 6g, Fat: 5g

Fiber: 4g

30. AIR FRYER SPICED POTATO WEDGES

Prep Time: 10 mins
Cook Time: 15 mins
Total Time: 25 mins
Servings: 4

Ingredients:

- 2 Big russet potatoes, slice into wedges
- 1 tbsp olive oil
- ½ tsp salt
- ½ tsp smoked paprika
- ½ tsp garlic powder
- ¼ tsp black pepper
- ¼ tsp cayenne pepper (non-compulsory)

Instructions:

1. Set the air fryer's temperature to 400°F, or 200°C.
2. Add olive oil, salt, paprika, garlic powder, black pepper, and cayenne pepper to the potato wedges.
3. Arrange in a single layer in the air fryer basket.
4. Cook, shaking the basket halfway through, for 15 mins.

Nutrition (per serving):

Cals: 160, Carbs: 30g

Protein: 4g, Fat: 4g

Fiber: 3g

31. AIR FRYER CORN ON THE COB

Prep Time: 5 mins
Cook Time: 10 mins
Total Time: 15 mins
Servings: 4

Ingredients:

- 4 ears of corn, husked
- 2 tbsp butter, dilute
- ½ tsp salt
- ¼ tsp black pepper
- ½ tsp smoked paprika (non-compulsory)

Instructions:

1. Set the air fryer's temperature to 375°F, or 190°C.
2. Add salt, pepper, and smoked paprika to the corn after brushing it with dilute butter.
3. Cook the corn in the basket of the air fryer for ten mins, rotating it halfway through.
4. Take out, let it cool a little, and serve hot.

Nutrition (Per Serving):

Cals: 130, Carbs: 25g

Protein: 3g, Fat: 4g

Fiber: 3g

32. AIR FRYER CRISPY TOFU BITES

Prep Time: 10 mins
Cook Time: 15 mins
Total Time: 25 mins
Servings: 4

Ingredients:

- 1 block (14 oz) extra-firm tofu, pressed and cubed
- 1 tbsp soy sauce
- 1 tbsp cornstarch
- 1 tbsp olive oil
- ½ tsp garlic powder
- ½ tsp paprika

Instructions:

1. Set the air fryer's temperature to 375°F, or 190°C.
2. Combine the tofu cubes, olive oil, cornstarch, garlic powder, and paprika in a bowl.
3. Place in a single layer in the air fryer basket.
4. Shake the basket midway through the cooking time of 12 to 15 mins.
5. With dipping sauce, serve hot.

Nutrition (Per Serving):

Cals: 180, Carbs: 7g

Protein: 14g, Fat: 12g

Fiber: 2g

33. AIR FRYER ROASTED CHICKPEA SALAD

Prep Time: 10 mins
Cook Time: 15 mins
Total Time: 25 mins
Servings: 4

Ingredients:

- 1 can (15 oz) chickpeas, drained and rinsed
- 1 tbsp olive oil
- ½ tsp salt
- ½ tsp smoked paprika
- ¼ tsp garlic powder
- 4 cups of combined greens
- ½ cup cherry tomatoes, halved

- ¼ red onion, split
- ¼ cup feta cheese (non-compulsory)
- 2 tbsp balsamic dressing

Instructions:

1. Set the air fryer's temperature to 375°F, or 190°C.
2. Add paprika, garlic powder, salt, and olive oil to the chickpeas.
3. Place in the air fryer basket in a single layer and cook, shaking occasionally, for 12 to 15 mins.
4. Put the greens, feta, tomatoes, onion, and crispy chickpeas in a bowl.
5. Serve with a balsamic dressing drizzle.

Nutrition (Per Serving):

Cals: 230, Carbs: 25g

Protein: 7g, Fat: 12g

Fiber: 6g

34. AIR FRYER STUFFED GRAPE LEAVES

Prep Time: 20 mins
Cook Time: 12 mins
Total Time: 32 mins
Servings: 6

Ingredients:

- 20 grape leaves, rinsed
- 1 cup cooked rice
- ½ cup chop-up parsley
- ¼ cup diced onion
- 1 tbsp lemon juice
- 1 tsp olive oil
- ½ tsp salt
- ½ tsp black pepper

Instructions:

1. Rice, parsley, onion, lemon juice, olive oil, salt, and pepper Must all be combined in a bowl.
2. Roll every grape leaf firmly after adding 1 tsp of filling.
3. Set the air fryer's temperature to 175°C (350°F).
4. Arrange the grape leaves in a single layer in the basket of the air fryer after lightly spraying it with oil.

5. Cook, turning halfway through, for 10 to 12 mins.
6. Warm up and serve with tzatziki or yogurt.

Nutrition (Per Serving):

Cals: 120, Carbs: 18g

Protein: 3g, Fat: 4g

Fiber: 3g

35. AIR FRYER CHEESY CAULIFLOWER BITES

Prep Time: 15 mins
Cook Time: 12 mins
Total Time: 27 mins
Servings: 4

Ingredients:

- 2 cups of cauliflower florets
- ½ cup shredded cheddar cheese
- ¼ cup breadcrumbs
- 1 egg, beaten
- ½ tsp garlic powder
- ½ tsp salt
- ¼ tsp black pepper

Instructions:

1. Set the air fryer's temperature to 375°F, or 190°C.
2. Add the cauliflower, cheese, breadcrumbs, egg, salt, pepper, and garlic powder to a bowl.
3. Put them in the basket of the air fryer after forming them into little, bite-sized balls.
4. Cook up to golden and crispy, 10 to 12 mins.
5. With dipping sauce, serve hot.

Nutrition (Per Serving):

Cals: 150, Carbs: 10g

Protein: 9g, Fat: 8g

Fiber: 3g

36. AIR FRYER FRIED ICE CREAM

Prep Time: 15 mins (+ freezing)
Cook Time: 5 mins
Total Time: 4 hrs 20 mins
Servings: 4

Ingredients:

- 4 scoops vanilla ice cream
- 2 cups of cornflakes, crushed
- 1 tsp cinnamon
- 2 tbsp butter, dilute
- 2 tbsp sugar
- 1 egg
- 1 tbsp milk
- Honey, chocolate syrup, or caramel (for serving)

Instructions:

1. Place the scooped ice cream in balls on a parchment paper-lined baking sheet. For at least two hrs, freeze.
2. Combine sugar, dilute butter, cinnamon, and crushed cornflakes in a bowl.
3. Whisk the egg and milk together in a separate dish.
4. Coat the refrigerate ice cream balls with the cornflake Mixture after rolling them in the egg Mixture. For a double coating, repeat.
5. For at least two more hrs, freeze once more.
6. Set the air fryer's temperature to 400°F, or 200°C.
7. The coated ice cream balls Must be cooked for four to five mins, or up to golden brown, in the air fryer basket.
8. Before serving, drizzle with caramel, chocolate syrup, or honey.

Nutrition (per serving):

Cals: 280, Protein: 4g

Carbs: 42g

Fat: 12g, Sugar: 24g

37. AIR FRYER PUMPKIN SPICE DONUTS

Prep Time: 10 mins
Cook Time: 8 mins
Total Time: 18 mins
Servings: 6

Ingredients:

- 1 cup all-purpose flour
- ½ cup pumpkin purée
- ¼ cup brown sugar
- 1 tsp pumpkin spice
- 1 tsp baking powder
- ½ tsp baking soda
- ¼ tsp salt
- 1 egg
- 2 tbsp dilute butter
- 2 tbsp milk
- 1 tsp vanilla extract
- For Coating:
- ¼ cup sugar
- 1 tsp cinnamon
- 2 tbsp dilute butter

Instructions:

1. Set the air fryer's temperature to 175°C (350°F).
2. Combine the flour, baking soda, baking powder, salt, and pumpkin spice in a bowl.
3. Whisk the egg, butter, milk, vanilla, brown sugar, and pumpkin purée in a separate basin.
4. Combine the wet components into the dry ingredients gradually up to they are well blended.
5. Pipe the batter into a greased donut shape after transferring it to a piping bag.
6. Cook in an air fryer for 8 mins, or up to cooked through and golden.
7. In a bowl, combine sugar and cinnamon. Coat the heated donuts with the cinnamon-sugar Mixture after brushing them with dilute butter.
8. Warm up and serve.

Nutrition (per donut):

Cals: 160, Protein: 3g

Carbs: 26g

Fat: 5g, Sugar: 12g

38. AIR FRYER COCONUT MACAROONS

Prep Time: 10 mins
Cook Time: 10 mins
Total Time: 20 mins
Servings: 12

Ingredients:

- 2 cups of shredded coconut
- ½ cup sweetened condensed milk
- 1 tsp vanilla extract
- 2 egg whites
- ¼ tsp salt
- ½ cup chocolate chips (non-compulsory, for dipping)

Instructions:

1. Set the air fryer's temperature to 325°F, or 160°C.
2. Combine the vanilla essence, sweetened condensed milk, and shredded coconut in a bowl.
3. Beat the egg whites and salt in a another bowl up to firm peaks form.
4. The egg whites Must be gently folded into the coconut Mixture.
5. Spoon little spoonfuls into an air fryer basket coated with paper.
6. Air fried till golden brown, 8 to 10 mins.
7. Let to cool fully. Dip the bottoms in dilute chocolate and let them set if you'd like.
8. Serve and savor!

Nutrition (per macaroon):

Cals: 100, Protein: 1g

Carbs: 10g

Fat: 6g, Sugar: 8g

39. AIR FRYER CINNAMON SUGAR DONUTS

Prep Time: 10 mins
Cook Time: 8 mins
Total Time: 18 mins
Servings: 8 donuts

Ingredients:

- 1 can (16 oz) refrigerated biscuit dough
- 2 tbsp dilute butter
- ½ cup granulated sugar
- 1 tsp ground cinnamon

Instructions:

1. Set the air fryer's temperature to 175°C (350°F).
2. Use a little sliceter or bottle cap to make holes in the middle of every biscuit.
3. Make sure to leave room between the donuts and holes when placing them in the air fryer basket.

4. Cook in the air fryer for 6 to 8 mins, turning halfway through, up to golden brown.
5. Coat in cinnamon sugar and brush with dilute butter while still heated.
6. Warm up and dig in!

Nutrition (per donut):

Cals: 180, Carbs: 25g

Protein: 3g, Fat: 8g

Sugar: 10g

40. AIR FRYER BANANA CHIPS

Prep Time: 5 mins
Cook Time: 15 mins
Total Time: 20 mins
Servings: 2

Ingredients:

- 2 ripe bananas, split thin
- 1 tbsp lemon juice
- ½ tsp cinnamon (non-compulsory)

Instructions:

1. Set the air fryer's temperature to 300°F, or 150°C.
2. To keep banana slices from browning, toss them with lemon juice.
3. Place in the basket of the air fryer in a single layer.
4. Air fried up to crisp, turning halfway through, 10 to 15 mins.
5. Enjoy after letting cool to crisp up even more!

Nutrition (per serving):

Cals: 110, Carbs: 28g

Protein: 1g, Fat: 0g

Sugar: 14g

41. AIR FRYER STRAWBERRY SHORTCAKE

Prep Time: 15 mins
Cook Time: 10 mins
Total Time: 25 mins
Servings: 4

Ingredients:

- 1 can refrigerated biscuit dough
- 1 tbsp dilute butter
- 1 cup strawberries, split
- 2 tbsp sugar
- 1 cup whipped cream

Instructions:

1. Set the air fryer's temperature to 175°C (350°F).
2. Melt the butter on the biscuits and air fry them for 8 to 10 mins, or up to they are golden brown.
3. Let strawberries rest for ten mins after tossing them with sugar.
4. Slice biscuits in half, then cover with whipped cream and strawberries.
5. Serve right away.

Nutrition (per serving):

Cals: 220, Carbs: 30g

Protein: 3g, Fat: 10g

Sugar: 12g

42. AIR FRYER S'MORES

Prep Time: 5 mins
Cook Time: 4 mins
Total Time: 9 mins
Servings: 4

Ingredients:

- 4 graham crackers, broken in half
- 4 Big marshmlets
- 4 pieces of chocolate

Instructions:

1. Turn the air fryer on to 370°F, or 190°C.
2. Put the halves of graham crackers in the air fryer basket and place a marshmlet on top.
3. The marshmlets Must be golden after 3-4 mins in the air fryer.
4. Take out, place another half of a graham cracker on top, and then add a piece of chocolate.
5. Warm up and dig in!

Nutrition (per s'more):

Cals: 150, Carbs: 28g

Protein: 2g, Fat: 5g

Sugar: 18g

43. AIR FRYER VEGAN TACOS

Prep Time: 10 mins
Cook Time: 15 mins
Total Time: 25 mins
Servings: 4

Ingredients:

- 8 ozs tempeh, cut up
- 1 tbsp olive oil
- 1 tsp chili powder
- 1/2 tsp ground cumin
- 1/2 tsp salt
- 8 mini corn tortillas
- 1 cup shredded lettuce
- 1/2 cup diced tomatoes
- 1/4 cup diced onions
- 1/4 cup chop-up cilantro
- Lime wedges, for serving

Instructions:

1. To prepare the tempeh, combine the cut up tempeh, salt, cumin, chili powder, and olive oil in a dish and toss up to well coated.
2. Air-Fry the Tempeh: Set the air fryer's temperature to 325°F (163°C). Arrange the seasoned tempeh in a single layer within the air fryer basket. Cook up to the tempeh is brown and crispy, shaking the basket halfway through. This Must take ten to fifteen mins.
3. Put the tacos together: Use a microwave or a skillet to reheat the corn tortillas. Top with chop-up tomatoes, cilantro, and shredded lettuce after stuffing every tortilla with a piece of the air-fried tempeh. Lime wedges Must be served alongside.

Nutrition (per serving):

Cals: 250, Protein: 12g, Carbs: 28g

Fat: 12g, Saturated Fat: 2g, Sodium: 400mg

Fiber: 5g, Sugar: 2g

44. AIR FRYER TEMPEH STIR FRY

Prep Time: 20 mins
Cook Time: 20 mins
Total Time: 40 mins
Servings: 4

Ingredients:

- 1 block (8 ozs) tempeh, slice into 1-inch cubes
- 1 tbsp low-sodium soy sauce
- 1 tsp sesame oil
- 1 tbsp olive oil
- 1/2 tsp salt
- 1/2 tsp garlic powder
- 1/2 tsp onion powder
- 1/4 tsp black pepper
- 3-4 tbsp cornstarch
- 1 red bell pepper, split
- 1 cup broccoli florets
- 1/2 cup split carrots
- 1/2 cup split onions
- 1/4 cup low-sodium soy sauce
- 2 tbsp hoisin sauce
- 1 tsp finely grated fresh ginger
- 1 clove garlic, chop-up
- Cooked rice or noodles, for serving

Instructions:

1. Marinate the tempeh by combining the cubes of tempeh with 1 tbsp of soy sauce, sesame oil, olive oil, salt, onion powder, black pepper, and garlic powder in a bowl. Toss to ensure even coating. Give it ten mins to marinate.
2. Apply Cornstarch: Drizzle the marinated tempeh with cornstarch and toss to coat every piece well.
3. Air-Fry the Tempeh: Set the air fryer's temperature to 375°F, or 190°C. Arrange the tempeh in a single layer within the air fryer basket. Cook up to the tempeh is brown and crispy, shaking the basket halfway through the 15 mins.
4. Get the vegetables ready: Steam or microwave the broccoli and carrots up to they are crisp-tender while the tempeh cooks.
5. Stir-Fry the Vegetables: Saute the red bell pepper and onions in a Big pan over medium heat up to they are tender. To the skillet, add the carrots and broccoli that have been steam-cooked.

6. Add Sauce and Tempeh: After the tempeh is cooked, combine it with the veggies in the skillet. Combine the hoisin sauce, finely grated ginger, chop-up garlic, and 1/4 cup soy sauce in a mini bowl. Coat the tempeh and veggies equally with the sauce by pouring it over them and stirring. Cook for a further two to three mins, or up to well heated.
7. Serve: Top the stir-fried tempeh with cooked noodles or rice.

Nutrition (per serving):

Cals: 300, Protein: 15g, Carbs: 35g

Fat: 12g, Saturated Fat: 2g, Sodium: 800mg

Fiber: 5g, Sugar: 6g

45. AIR FRYER CHOCOLATE LAVA CAKE

Prep Time: 10 mins
Cook Time: 8 mins
Total Time: 18 mins
Servings: 2

Ingredients

- ½ cup semi-sweet chocolate chips
- ¼ cup unsalted butter
- 1 egg
- 1 egg yolk
- ¼ cup powdered sugar
- 2 tbsp all-purpose flour
- ¼ tsp vanilla extract
- Pinch of salt

Instructions

1. Set the air fryer's temperature to 375°F, or 190°C. Coat two ramekins with oil.
2. In a bowl that may be placed in the microwave, melt the butter and chocolate together. Combine up to it's smooth.
3. Whisk together the egg, egg yolk, salt, vanilla, and powdered sugar in a separate basin.
4. Fold in the flour after stirring in the dilute chocolate Mixture.
5. After dividing the batter among the ramekins, put them in the air fryer.
6. The middle Must be somewhat runny but the edges Must be firm after 7 to 8 mins in the air fryer.
7. Before turning into plates, let it settle for a min. Warm up and serve.

Nutrition (Per Serving)

Cals: 310 | Carbs: 32g | Protein: 5g | Fat: 19g

46. AIR FRYER CHURROS

Prep Time: 15 mins
Cook Time: 10 mins
Total Time: 25 mins
Servings: 12 churros

Ingredients

- ½ cup water
- 2 tbsp unsalted butter
- 1 tbsp sugar
- ¼ tsp salt
- ½ cup all-purpose flour
- 1 egg
- ½ tsp vanilla extract
- ½ cup sugar + 1 tsp cinnamon (for coating)
- Cooking spray

Instructions

1. Bring the water, butter, sugar, and salt to a boil in a saucepan.
2. After taking off the heat, combine in the flour up to a dough forms. Give it five mins to cool.
3. Add vanilla and egg and stir up to smooth. Spoon dough into a star-tipped piping bag.
4. After piping the churros onto parchment paper, air fried them for 8 to 10 mins at 375°F (190°C).
5. Serve the heated churros after tossing them in cinnamon and sugar.

Nutrition (Per Churro)

Cals: 85 | Carbs: 12g | Protein: 1g | Fat: 3g

47. AIR FRYER APPLE HAND PIES

Prep Time: 15 mins
Cook Time: 12 mins
Total Time: 27 mins
Servings: 4

Ingredients

- 1 refrigerated pie crust, rolled out
- 1 cup apple pie filling, chop-up

- 1 egg (for egg wash)
- 1 tbsp sugar
- ½ tsp cinnamon

Instructions

1. Set the air fryer's temperature to 350°F (175°C).
2. Make four 5-inch rounds out of the pie crust.
3. On one edge of every circle, spoon apple filling.
4. Using a fork, secure the edges after folding over. Apply egg wash to the brush.
5. Air fried till golden brown, 10 to 12 mins.
6. Sprinkle over the pies after combining the sugar and cinnamon.

Nutrition (Per Pie)

Cals: 220 | Carbs: 35g | Protein: 3g | Fat: 9g

48. AIR FRYER BROWNIES

Prep Time: 10 mins
Cook Time: 15 mins
Total Time: 25 mins
Servings: 6

Ingredients

- ½ cup unsalted butter, dilute
- ½ cup sugar
- ¼ cup brown sugar
- 1 egg
- ½ tsp vanilla extract
- ½ cup all-purpose flour
- ¼ cup cocoa powder
- ¼ tsp salt
- ¼ tsp baking powder
- ½ cup chocolate chips

Instructions

1. Turn the air fryer on to 320°F, or 160°C.
2. Combine the butter, sugars, egg, and vanilla in a bowl.
3. Add baking powder, flour, cocoa powder, and salt and sift. Combine up to incorporated.
4. Add chocolate chips and fold.
5. Fill a 6-inch baking pan that has been oiled with batter.
6. For fifteen mins, air fry. Before slicing, let cool.

Nutrition (Per Serving)

Cals: 250 | Carbs: 32g | Protein: 3g | Fat: 13g

49. AIR FRYER PEANUT BUTTER COOKIES

Prep Time: 10 mins
Cook Time: 8 mins
Total Time: 18 mins
Servings: 12 cookies

Ingredients

- ½ cup peanut butter
- ¼ cup sugar
- ¼ cup brown sugar
- 1 egg
- ½ tsp vanilla extract
- ½ cup all-purpose flour
- ½ tsp baking soda
- Pinch of salt

Instructions

1. Set the air fryer's temperature to 350°F (175°C).
2. Combine peanut butter, sugars, egg, and vanilla in a bowl.
3. Add salt, baking soda, and flour and stir up to dough forms.
4. Roll into 1-inch balls and use a fork to gently flatten.
5. For 7 to 8 mins, air fry. Before serving, let to cool.

Nutrition (Per Cookie)

Cals: 120 | Carbs: 10g | Protein: 3g | Fat: 8g

50. ZEMIAKOVÝ GULÁŠ S ZELENINOU (POTATO GOULASH WITH VEGETABLES)

Prep Time: 20 mins

Cook Time: 40 mins

Total Time: 1 hr

Servings: 6

Ingredients:

- 4 potatoes, peel off and diced
- 2 carrots, split
- 1 onion, diced
- 2 cloves garlic, chop-up
- 2 tbsp tomato paste
- 4 cups of vegetable broth
- 1 tsp paprika
- 1 tsp dried thyme
- Salt and pepper as needed
- 2 tbsp olive oil
- Chop-up fresh parsley for garnish

Instructions:

1. Heat the olive oil in a Big saucepan over medium heat. After adding the chop-up onion and garlic, simmer for three to four mins, or up to the ingredients are tender.
2. For a further five mins, simmer the split carrots and diced potatoes, stirring occasionally.
3. Stir in the tomato paste, paprika, and dry thyme up to thoroughly combined.
4. Bring the Mixture to a boil after adding the vegetable broth. Cover and simmer for 20 to 25 mins once the potatoes and carrots are tender.
5. Season with salt and pepper as needed.
6. Serve hot, garnished with freshly chop-up parsley.

NUTRITION INFO: (per serving)

Cals: 180, Protein: 4g

Fat: 4g, Carbs: 30g

Fiber: 4g

51. KUSHARI DELIGHT

Prep Time: 20 mins
Cook Time: 40 mins
Total Time: 1 hr
Servings: 4

Ingredients:

- 1 cup dried lentils
- 1 cup rice
- 1 cup elbow macaroni
- 1 cup cooked chickpeas
- 1 cup tomato sauce

- 1/4 cup olive oil
- 1 onion, lightly chop-up
- 3 cloves garlic, chop-up
- 1 tsp cumin
- Salt and pepper as needed

Instructions:
1. Prepare lentils as directed on the packet.
2. Prepare the macaroni and rice in a different pot per the directions on the box/pkg.
3. Add the chop-up garlic and chop-up onions to a big skillet and cook in olive oil up to golden brown.
4. Season the pan with salt, pepper, cumin, and tomato sauce. Simmer for ten mins.
5. Add the rice, macaroni, chickpeas, and cooked lentils to the pan with the tomato sauce Mixture. Stir well.
6. Enjoy your Kushari Delight while it's still hot!

Nutrition:
Cals: 450 per serving

Protein: 15g, Carbs: 75g

Fat: 10g

52. FAVA BEAN FALAFEL

Prep Time: 15 mins
Cook Time: 20 mins
Total Time: 35 mins
Servings: 6

Ingredients:
- 2 cups of cooked fava beans
- 1 onion, chop-up
- 3 cloves garlic, chop-up
- 1/2 cup fresh parsley, chop-up
- 1 tsp cumin
- 1 tsp coriander
- Salt and pepper as needed
- 1/4 cup flour
- 1/4 cup olive oil for frying

Instructions:

1. Process the fava beans, onion, garlic, parsley, cumin, coriander, salt, and pepper in a mixer up to they are smooth.
2. Move the Mixture to a bowl and combine in the flour up to it's thoroughly combined in.
3. Create little patties out of the Mixture.
4. In a skillet over medium heat, heat the olive oil and cook the falafel up to golden brown on both sides.
1. Drain on paper towels and serve hot.

Nutrition:

Cals: 200 per serving

Protein: 8g, Carbs: 25g, Fat: 8g

53. ALEXANDRIA SEAFOOD STEW

Prep Time: 30 mins
Cook Time: 40 mins
Total Time: 1 hr 10 mins
Servings: 4

Ingredients:

- 1 lb combined seafood (shrimp, mussels, fish)
- 2 tbsp olive oil
- 1 onion, chop-up
- 3 cloves garlic, chop-up
- 1 can diced tomatoes
- 1 cup fish or vegetable broth
- 1/2 cup white wine
- 1 tsp dried oregano
- Salt and pepper as needed
- Fresh parsley for garnish

Instructions:

1. Heat the olive oil in a big saucepan and cook the chop-up garlic and chop-up onions up to they are tender.
2. Include oregano, white wine, chop-up tomatoes, fish or vegetable broth, salt, and pepper. For 20 mins, simmer.
3. Cook the combined seafood up to it is thoroughly done.
4. Serve hot, garnished with fresh parsley.

Nutrition:

Cals: 300 per serving

Protein: 20g, Carbs: 10g, Fat: 15g

54. EGYPTIAN LENTIL SOUP

Prep Time: 15 mins
Cook Time: 30 mins
Total Time: 45 mins
Servings: 6

Ingredients:

- 1 cup dried red lentils
- 1 onion, chop-up
- 2 carrots, diced
- 2 cloves garlic, chop-up
- 1 tsp cumin
- 1 tsp coriander
- 6 cups of vegetable broth
- Salt and pepper as needed
- Juice of 1 lemon
- Fresh cilantro for garnish

Instructions:

1. Use cold water to rinse the lentils.
2. Saute the chop-up garlic, split carrots, and chop-up onions in a big saucepan up to they are tender.
3. Include the vegetable broth, lentils, cumin, coriander, salt, and pepper. For 20 mins, simmer.
4. Blend the soup up to it's smooth using an immersion blender.
5. Before serving, stir in lemon juice and sprinkle with fresh cilantro.

Nutrition:

Cals: 180 per serving

Protein: 10g, Carbs: 30g, Fat: 3g

55. KOFTA KEBABS WITH TZATZIKI

Prep Time: 20 mins
Cook Time: 15 mins
Total Time: 35 mins
Servings: 4

Ingredients:

- 1 lb ground lamb or beef
- 1 mini onion, lightly chop-up
- 2 cloves garlic, chop-up
- 1/4 cup breadcrumbs
- 1 tsp ground cumin
- 1 tsp ground coriander
- Salt and pepper as needed
- Wooden skewers, soaked in water

Tzatziki Sauce:

- 1 cup Greek yogurt
- 1 cucumber, finely grated and drained
- 2 cloves garlic, chop-up
- 1 tbsp olive oil
- 1 tbsp fresh dill, chop-up
- Salt and pepper as needed

Instructions:

1. Put the breadcrumbs, cumin, coriander, chop-up garlic, chop-up onion, ground beef, salt, and pepper in a bowl. Combine together and shape into little, long kebabs.
2. Attach the kebabs to the wooden skewers that have been moistened.
3. For approximately 12 to 15 mins, grill or broil the kebabs, rotating them often, up to they are cooked through.
4. In a bowl, combine Greek yogurt, finely grated cucumber, olive oil, chop-up garlic, dill, salt, and pepper to make the tzatziki sauce.
5. Present the kofta kebabs beside tzatziki sauce.

Nutrition:

(Per serving, without pita or additional sides)

Cals: 300, Protein: 25g

Carbs: 8g

Fat: 18g

56. HAWAWSHI - MEAT-STUFFED PITA

Prep Time: 15 mins
Cook Time: 25 mins

Total Time: 40 mins
Servings: 6

Ingredients:

- 1 lb ground beef or lamb
- 1 onion, lightly chop-up
- 2 tomatoes, diced
- 1/4 cup parsley, chop-up
- 1 tsp ground cumin
- 1 tsp ground coriander
- Salt and pepper as needed
- 6 pita bread rounds

Instructions:

1. Cook the ground beef in a pan up to it turns golden. Take out extra fat.
2. Include the diced tomatoes, chop-up onion, parsley, coriander, cumin, salt, and pepper. Simmer up to the onions are tender.
3. Set the oven's temperature to 175°C (350°F).
4. Stuff the meat Mixture into a pocket slice out of every pita bread.
5. Put the filled pitas on a baking pan and bake them for ten to twelve mins.

Nutrition:(Per serving)

Cals: 320, Protein: 20g

Carbs: 25g

Fat: 15g

57. MOLOKHIA GREEN SOUP

Prep Time: 30 mins
Cook Time: 40 mins
Total Time: 1 hr 10 mins
Servings: 8

Ingredients:

- 2 cups of dry molokhia leaves (jute leaves), chop-up
- 1 lb chicken, slice into pieces
- 1 onion, lightly chop-up
- 3 cloves garlic, chop-up
- 4 cups of chicken broth
- 1 lemon, juiced
- Salt and pepper as needed

- Olive oil for drizzling

Instructions:
1. Saute the garlic and onions in olive oil in a saucepan up to they are tender.
2. After adding the chicken pieces, brown them on all sides.
3. Bring to a simmer after adding the chicken broth.
4. Simmer for 30 to 40 mins after adding the chop-up molokhia leaves.
5. Add lemon juice, salt, and pepper for seasoning.
6. Before serving, drizzle with olive oil.

Nutrition:(Per serving)

Cals: 180, Protein: 15g

Carbs: 10g, Fat: 8g

58. BASBOUSA - SEMOLINA CAKE

Prep Time: 15 mins
Cook Time: 30 mins
Total Time: 45 mins
Servings: 12

Ingredients:
- 1 cup semolina
- 1 cup plain yogurt
- 1 cup granulated sugar
- 1 cup desiccated coconut
- 1/2 cup unsalted butter, dilute
- 1 tsp baking powder
- 1 tsp vanilla extract
- Slivered almonds for garnish

Syrup:
- 1 cup granulated sugar
- 1/2 cup water
- 1 tbsp lemon juice

Instructions:
1. Set the oven's temperature to 175°C (350°F). Coat a baking dish with oil.
2. Combine yogurt, sugar, desiccated coconut, dilute butter, baking powder, vanilla essence, and semolina in a dish.
3. Smooth the top of the batter after pouring it into the prepared dish.

4. Bake up to golden brown, 25 to 30 mins.
5. Make the syrup by heating the sugar, water, and lemon juice up to they slightly thicken while the cake bakes.
6. Cover the cake with the hot syrup when it's finished.
7. Before serving, add split almonds as a garnish and let them to absorb the syrup.

Nutrition:(Per serving)

Cals: 280, Protein: 4g

Carbs: 40g

Fat: 12g

59. TAHINI HONEY ROASTED CARROTS

Prep Time: 10 mins

Cook Time: 25 mins

Total Time: 35 mins

Servings: 4

Ingredients:

- 1 lb baby carrots, washed and peel off
- 2 tbsp olive oil
- 2 tbsp honey
- 2 tbsp tahini
- Salt and pepper as needed
- Fresh parsley for garnish (non-compulsory)

Instructions:

1. Set the oven's temperature to 400°F, or 200°C.
2. Combine the tahini, honey, and olive oil in a bowl and whisk to combine.
3. Coat the young carrots evenly by tossing them in the Mixture.
4. Arrange the carrots in a single layer on a baking pan.
5. Add salt and pepper for seasoning.
6. The carrots Must be soft and beginning to caramelize after 25 mins of roasting in a preheated oven.
7. If preferred, garnish with fresh parsley.
8. Serve and savor!

NUTRITION INFO (per serving):

Cals: 150, Protein: 2g

Fat: 8g, Carbs: 20g

Fiber: 4g

60. SHISH TAOUK SKEWERS

Prep Time: 20 mins

Cook Time: 15 mins

Total Time: 35 mins

Servings: 6

Ingredients:

- 1.5 lbs boneless, skinless chicken breast, slice into cubes
- 1/4 cup plain yogurt
- 3 tbsp olive oil
- 2 tbsp tomato paste
- 2 cloves garlic, chop-up
- 1 tsp ground cumin
- 1 tsp paprika
- 1 tsp turmeric
- Salt and pepper as needed
- Wooden skewers, soaked in water

Instructions:

1. To make the marinade, combine yogurt, olive oil, tomato paste, turmeric, paprika, cumin, garlic, and salt and pepper in a bowl.
2. Coat the chicken cubes equally after adding them to the marinade. For at least an hr, or better yet, overnight, marinate.
3. Heat the grill or grill pan to a temperature of medium-high.
4. Put chunks of marinated chicken on skewers.
5. The chicken Must be cooked through after 6 to 8 mins on every side of the grill skewers.
6. Serve with flatbread or rice.

NUTRITION INFO (per serving):

Cals: 250

Protein: 30g

Made in the USA
Columbia, SC
28 March 2025